A Moment of Attention

Chris Hardy

original plus

this collection 'A Moment of Attention'
first published in Britain by
'original plus'
17 High Street
Maryport,
Cumbria.   CA15 6BQ

ISBN 978-0-9546801-5-2

cover design/drawing by Martha Hardy

printed by original plus press
bound by PM Press

Some of these poems have appeared in the following publications and places:

Avocado; Brando's Hat; Brittle Star; Dreamcatcher; Fire; Frogmore Papers; www.greatworks.org.uk; Iota; London Writers Competition Prizewinners' anthologies; Moodswing; Neon Highway; Obsessed With Pipework; Orbis; Ore; Outlaw; Page 84; Pennine Platform; Planet; Poetry Monthly; Poetry Nottingham; www.poetrypf.co.uk; Pulsar; Seam; Smith's Knoll; South; Tears In The Fence; the Coffee House; the North; Voice and Verse; Weyfarers.

'The Wedding' was commended in a recent Poetry Society's National Poetry competition; 'Ikram' was a prizewinner in a recent Amnesty International competition; 'Without Stopping' and 'Somewhere To Go' were prize winners in recent London Writers competitions. 'Mrs Panayiotou's Place' was commended in a recent Ware Poets Competition. All were published in the respective competition's anthologies and/or on their websites.

about the author

Chris Hardy has been writing poetry for more than twenty years; his poems have appeared in over 60 magazines including Poetry Review, Stand, Agenda, Orbis, the North, Smith's Knoll, Tears in the Fence, Frogmore papers, Wasafiri, Staple, Slow Dancer, Oasis and Brando's Hat. Some have won prizes in magazine competitions and also in the National Poetry Society's and London Writers' poetry competitions. Poems have appeared in several anthologies eg New Poetry 5 (Art's Council, Ed. Jon Silkin). One collection, 'Swimming in the Deep Diamond Mine' has been published by Hub Editions.

Chris is also a musician and plays in the bluesrock band BIGROAD. A new CD of acoustic music, 'Health To Your Hands' will appear in Summer 2008.

For more information see:-
www.greatworks.org.uk
www.poetrypf.co.uk
http://www.myspace.com/mrchrishardy
www.bigroad.net
http://www.myspace.com/bigroadbluesbanduk

for Raphy and Isaac

contents

A Moment of Attention

The Wedding

Suddenly they were there a wall of men all singing
surging towards us down the lane
behind the harbour

one playing a guitar held high and secured by an elbow
in the center a young man
with a garland on his head

his face flushed led firmly by each arm
his father gripping one side
smaller than his son and stronger

with a harsh grey cut and a face as red
as the plug of wet grape skins
we'd seen him throw to the goat.

A groom on his way to a bride
befuddled and unsteady
with a dazed grin.

Wounded soldiers slugged with brandy
then rushed to the surgeon
carelessness rising in their cheeks

or youths dragged to the gallows drunk
a laugh quivering round their lips
not really knowing

must have looked the same
though this groom knew
and was not afraid

just surprised
that this famous performance
was now his.

Round the corner the girls step from their cars
raise their long white skirts
bend, remove their heels

then holding back their veils
bare-legged run through the dust
flickering like moths in the dark

to the chapel on the shore
crammed with golden candle-light
like a beehive,

where we'd stopped the night before in a storm
to ask Mary though we were asking the sea
to help us get away and go home.

The Word Life In Red

Full size
in a black frame
the sky stands up
suspending tall white clouds.
It's mid-afternoon
in Summer
somewhere near Flagstaff
Arizona.
The highway slides uphill
and forward
out of the picture
past a hitchhiker
who waits to ride
from this nameless place
to California.

A Motel, a Diner selling
burgers and Coke,
a garage for the truck
and the Pontiac
just pulling out,
check the oil
wipe the windscreen
dollar gas.
Andreas Feininger
took this
black and white photo
of Route 66 in '53.
Next to his name
is printed
the word LIFE
in red.

Second Trimester

You are careful to be happy
impossible to rile

as if you are listening
to someone else.

We cannot approach or trouble
your focus

we have been left behind
in a lesser life

where everything still goes on
and is nothing.

You have become as precise
as your pear-tight belly

from which you have removed
the silver ring

inserted once to shock us –
it didn't work –

or to entice yourself
or another.

The decks are stripped
for action.

Jenny

She has hung there for some time.
I thought a photograph of my grandmother
as a pretty young woman
looking to her left
a sort of flattery to me.

Then her daughter said
the reason she sits like that
arms falling to her hands
folded in her lap
her gaze slightly lowered

is to conceal her pregnancy
which was not considered a
respectable enough condition
to hang on any wall even
her own.

Eyeglass

A mirror forgets
immediately
like an old man who

doesn't know his old
wife's face looking down
at 3pm

but still can see
his son's new face
one long gone dawn.

A mirror's eye
is always young
it needs no specs

but when it cracks
its useless, nothing
can be done

although the tall
glass triangles
must be beaten

into icy grain
before they're
blind.

Libation

We came back, called
across the sea
and Europe quickly
as we could

from Agrigento
zoccolo duro
hard hoof
of the Mafia where

concrete high-rise
smothers churches
and edges slowly but
without a pause

towards the temples
where they stand
above the shore
buttressed fragile
honeycomb.

Your waters broke, the sun shone
on your sister as she asked
Hera, Herakles and Zeus
with drops upon the ground

to help you face your first
surely these gods even if they're
dried up like the grass
and whisper like a cricket

familiar with our pleading
for health revenge good luck
more pay could help but the sun
still, merciless unblinking
was in control that day.

You shivered, cried
drugged spiked and cut
so no one died
except your life before

you'll never be
my child again
a mother masters
every man,

in your own mother's arms
rescued sedate
your implored son
like a shelled cob waits
to claim you from yourself.

The Daughter Who Gave In

A friend
traveled in Afghanistan
and came back with
watercolours of Herat
a brown rampart along a ridge
beneath a blue sky
and Mazar Sharif's
blue domes.

He sat in courtyards at night
with Afghanis in white rolled
headcloths and white gowns
smoking hashish
the sort that sweats wet
in a brown lump
grows a white mould
and stinks of camels.

With this
they drank mint tea.
In England he married a girl
with money
and complained about her
family's habit
of living life as an emptiness
between meals.

And they
complained about him
to their daughter
who gave in.
There was one anguished call
and a card
a red dust thumb whorl
across the stamp.

His mind fell off a cliff
like Buddha in Bamiyan
more lost in Surrey
than the desert
I forget the place
they put you in, somewhere
for those whose minds
wander.

The Man Who Hailed A Taxi
and Stopped A Hearse

So she took all the things he'd,
mostly, paid for and put them in a cab.
She said she wanted her own
front door and though she loved him
that was that.

He visited her in her new place
to fix things up and strip the floor
and worried how alone she seemed
and about the roads and cars and strangers
outside the door.

One afternoon he just dropped by
beneath her window he heard her cries
fearful he ran then stopped and thought.
In that alley he lost his past
like a ticket down a drain

and he felt like a stone, cold
and uncovered by the rain.
He turned and left, he shut the gate,
out in the street again he made
his first mistake.

Words Like Hounds

Words like hounds begin to hunt
the words that explain

a strangeness found in a word
and the chase ends by unearthing

once again the only thing
there is to say.

The sky is a dome because
of the sea's flat line,

life's blue curves are floored
by death's horizon.

I Work All Day

I work all day
in this small bar
by the sea.

We start by sweeping
the floor and cleaning
the tables.

Then we serve breakfast
carrying it across
from the kitchen.

The sun begins
to pour out heat
around midday.

We have to serve
soft drinks and juice
in the shade.

As the afternoon passes
we prepare so that when
the sun has fallen

down the inside of the sky
and approaches the mountain
we are ready for the people,

who sit silent when they watch
the horizon, and talk
when they watch each other.

Darkness appears
in the air like dye
in water.

Everyone is at the centre
of their own life,
a thing they cannot see

from the outside.
Even in the mirror
of a polished table

I do not see
my life only a face
which seems to know

but will not tell
me what I am
or why.

Let's return to that bar
where the sun's evening light
burns on the mountain

that we will never visit.
We can take the children
plan tomorrow

and the days after,
buy food on the way
and spend some time,

like emptying our pockets
for the waitress.
The money spent

does not come back
and our time like the sun's
liquid gold pours

into the cold tide
of the past that goes out
for ever.

Somewhere Is Always Better Than Nowhere

The guide book did not say
that the beach it praises
is lined with small concrete cabins
in dilapidated gardens
where the owners drink
eat and sleep away each summer.
The town, where the Romans landed
to compete in the games
is now a street selling jewellery,
The gold is bought in Frankfurt.
From it we make these fine earrings
and bracelets depicting Athena's owl,
the double axe, the dolphin
that saved Arion.

'Below the romantic Keep the beach
 with rocky outcrops
 is good for swimming and
 beneath the surface
 you can see traces
 of the ancient enceinte
 preceding Villhuardain's improvements'.
No mention of the urchins
lining every crevice,
scheisse on Aphrodite's foam,
a bar spreading drink and noise
north and south
and cans, oil, rope, chains dumped
from passing cruise liners,

but then
isn't somewhere
always better
than nowhere?

Argos

The Argive Heraion, sanctuary of Hera
Goddess of the people of Argos
lies across a terrace
on top of a low hill
rising above miles of orange trees.

From the remaining lines of stones
the city and the slack warm sea
flopping through reeds onto a narrow shore
can be seen across the plain.

I remember you
leaning back against a fallen column
praising the sharp cool morning light.
It was as if I'd washed my face and eyes
from the inside.

Purdah

They're threshing with horses above the track
driving a team of three a mule on the inside
round a tight hippodrome.

By the gate a locust tree shades the well
attended by a tethered donkey
and barbed whirling hornets.

The shepherds bring their own buckets
because what is beneath
a few nailed planks is theirs.

I look in every time I pass
to be admitted to a secret
that feels like a privilege.

Cool silence rings in the chamber's bell,
a circle of silver like the moon
hovers in a starless pool.

As I stare up at myself the sun
persistent as a cat tries to edge
into the cell where a cold bride
constantly renewed is locked away.

From the threshing floor the horses
walk down prick eared and streaming.
Sweat opens veins in the dust
and chaff along their sides.

The farmer hauls a slopping pail
tips it into a trough
pours the rest over his head
and slams the lid against the heat.

A sharp rap echoes across the hill
where stones and thistles grow
straight through a wired-up gate
and down a gully to the sea
sleeping restlessly in a bay
where the sun drinks
and drinks all day.

Piazza Marina

I took your picture
several times
standing before
the fountain veiled
by fern-like
dropping threads
of water.
I tried again,
you by the harbour
and the church,
St. Mary of the Chain,
framed by steps,
columns,
water, walls
and boats
shivering on the sea.

My father took
a picture of me
where slaves had once
been sold.
The film came back
but only trees
and the auction block
remained.
We fly like birds
from frame to frame,
I tried to catch you
so you would
abide like
water, walls,
islands, trees
and chains.

The Cow's Belly

The bay is like a coin
golden, still,
polished flat by a column
of windless air.
A stream spreads and sinks
into the warm salt depths,
Tamarisk lays shadows
upon its mercury surface.

Fish and kingfishers gather
where these waters meet.
A lady with a hat
also a parasol
hitches up her dress
shows her girdle, petticoat,
cools her toes in the shallows
as her son skims his net.

The shore dips beneath
lines of water that ripple
like a thumbed ream.
At first you can see
your feet, then the darkness
goes down to where
the Turkish fleet
lies broken.

A Moment of Attention

The barn built from boards nailed
to a frame like a boat.
The purlins slotted into the walls
of the house still firm
but the planks split, slipped.
On an August afternoon
the still air inside is cool,
warm fans of light spread out
in silence hung with dust.
The swallows which live in the rafters
shoot out of the open doors
to dive-bomb our black cat
crouching and ducking
on the porch roof.

A woman lived in the house alone
fetching water from the spring.
She stayed indoors and grew fat
in the firelight her face burning
her back cold.
I cleared a rats' nest
from beneath the stairs,
it took a day to smash her bed
and drag it out
a trail of wax inches thick led
from the bed-side down to the grate.
In the dump outside we found
broken crocks, a spoon and big green
Gilbey's empties.

After a hot day the roof cracks
like gunshot.
In the barn feathery patched
broken so light
that it might blow away
it's easy to know
that there is only now
that life is short
a moment of attention
and be full of life
and want to live
until you've had enough. This
is the easiest thing
to forget.

What's Happening

Trees grow through the verandah,
plants flower on the roof and
root in the floorboards.

Riddled with creepers and branches,
rooms thick with leaves, the house
hovers above the grass.

I see it here suddenly again
though it was
five hundred miles from the sea
in another country, another century.

I see it as clearly as
the key I hold out towards
the door which secures this place
I stay in now,

where the lights flash on
like memory to show
what's happening
will have happened.

Late Afternoon Sun

Late afternoon sun.
Terraces block off the breeze
and hold the air
like a warm pool
flooding the backyards.

We sit together in the doorway
the only place the sun still reaches,
back over the roof tops
into our room.

A few minutes rest, with
the shadows lengthening towards us
and the rooms behind
becoming cool and dark.

Cringle Street

A schoolgirl with a
mouth of wire descends to where
the tube trains choir in

their burrow, autumn rain hangs
curtains down the road, the sun

fires from its place low
on the horizon, never
the same face twice

each day new populated
their hours done they vanish,

tomorrow's legion
will appear, walk down the road
and be forgotten.

In Cringle Street three men park
a Nissan and set off through

the dark towards a
cliff of flats speckled with light.
There's no call for the

blue music round here he said,
she told me fuck off fuck off

twenty times like that.
Until you turn the corner
by the park you do

not see the bridge where this road
ends, then across the river

another begins.
We saw a comet once, pale
ghost peering from night's

cloak dusk after dusk then gone.
Ice wings open on windscreens.

Like The Sea Itself

You find a diamond
large uncut beyond price
and lock it away forever.

You can do anything or nothing.
Once they're done
the obituary's spiked.

The only people who weep
are the bereaved
they still have time.

You can't regret
what you can't remember
or forget.

A full span
might make you feel
you haven't wasted it

but you can only treasure
what you have or what you've done
while you're doing something.

Living eagerly
remembering the alternative
doesn't avert what is not an alternative.

The forever we will get
though more than dust
is as big and heartless as the night

and the only forever
that will suffice
we cannot have:

eternal bliss without boredom
or a fade-out to impersonal peace
but the only peace is personal.

The man who discovered anaesthetic
wasted his life just as
those who love his solace

waste theirs
there's nothing else
that can be done with it.

Buy life so you can drink it
or fish in it or dam it up
and you get back

an ungraspable river
running through your hands
as you stare.

Swimming is free
and water touches you
everywhere at once.

The photographs
of our long holiday
are small shining ripples

like pinned moths' wings
or a stream
cut and dried.

The whale can hear his heart
and the singing of his fellows
far off across the ocean.

The sound flows round and through them
along their salty veins
like the sea itself.

My father's eightieth birthday
is upon him and must be celebrated
a feat of endurance.

As he leaves the table
and in the street the sun falls
once more upon his head and heart

he will not regret
he will not remember
or forget.

Without Stopping

Just to say that we are not allowed to watch TV
because Kennedy and Khruschev are having a showdown.
Some parents have got their kids back home from school
but as you're in Borneo that's out.

We spent today firing paper pellets soaked in ink
at each other from behind our desks.
Our weapons are elastic bands tied together,
we are fearless and accurate.

Yesterday I was caught buying cigarettes in a shop.
I said I'd bought them for my Granny who
as you know is dying from a chest condition.
Luckily they didn't ask.

One punishment we've had was to fork the Head's lawn and
as we were doing this Cockroft put a tine through his foot.
He stood there for a while saying, *I can't move.*
Cockroft says he's going to be a doctor.

We've thought up a game but not how to practice it:
the plan is to wait at the top of the stairs
and when it's quiet run straight down and out
through the big doors and across the road

without stopping.

The Bombing Map

There is a map which shows where every bomb
that fell on London
landed.
I did not believe this could be done
even when I saw it
but the hoardings
that once stood where a quartet fell
on each corner of the Lavender Hill junction
with the Wandsworth road
are still there.

They used to fill these gaps with adverts
and petrol stations are a sure sign
of a hit.
This area has come up since those nights
when the Germans
veering left above the power station
dumped bombs they'd failed to scatter
on the docks.
Two minutes over London
lit up like a snake along its river.

There's a bathroom emporium
where the blast took out
several triple-decker Victorians
down to the basement.
It is now recommended that we wash
in deep and gleaming baths
shaped like the tub of Telemakhos
the first thing they found at Pylos
another city burnt from roof to ground
by enemies we've forgotten how to fear.

And this reminds me of my mother's friend
a little more than friend I gather, once,
who came back to his house
stuck in the side of a valley
with the sea in a wood below,
came back from the emaciated edge
four years in a Japanese prison camp,
and said thank God and America
and everyone
for the atom bomb.

The Spartans

1

Three owls with Spartan
hoplite faces
are in this cage.
Their stillness does not please
the holiday makers.

They prefer the Capucin
who plays in his prison
and the otters
crying for food on time
like their children.

2

We came back mid-afternoon
late enough for the
old white buildings
to have soaked up
the long sun's reach.

We were looking for a place
to turn aside
maybe for good.
Offshore lay the island where
the Spartans first gave into fear.

We stood in the shining road
ignored by whirling nets of swifts
thrown together along the rooftops.
The only sidesteps they took
were to re-aim.

Why is it so hard for us
to accept our fate
walking forward on the clay
when they embrace theirs
asleep on the air?

The Far Side Of The World

9.50 tube
all experts

look
but don't get caught.

A tall woman
in a short skirt

black tights
and short boots.

I consider the
political situation

and decide
if she looks in her mirror

she knows
I might look in her mirror.

Opposite
a letter is unfolded,

'*I enjoy country pursuits,
I perhaps have said too much*'.

This searching
is going on everywhere.

I try three stores
but cannot find that

Piraeus Rembetica
we saw last month.

Things vanish
when your back is turned.

Today my daughter left
for the far side of the world.

Ngosi

I hear American voices from next door
eager to say what they think
about their election and
who should lead their country
which debate is also mine
though I have no voice in it.

Then I recall that in Africa
once I saw a lake
inside an extinct volcano
a great round pool
deep below us
in a sheer brown crater.

Our truck tipped over in the dust
on the way there
the dirt roads were corrugated rock
but the steep cambers
gathered sand, we were pushed upright
by many cheerful hands.

I must have eaten something that day
five hundred miles from the sea
and talked to those who helped us out
I don't remember any of that just
a huge blue unblinking eye
looking up into the

clean clear
empty
sky.

Ikram

Ikram hides her face,
sits in the corner and will not raise
her head, she looks up
with her eyes alone.

She flies across the hurdles
in her long blue dress
and with her friends
begins to speak.

They gather and whirl
about each other
like bright clothes
blowing on a line.

We talk at her, say things
she cannot know and yet
she learns
like a desert hoarding rain.

Then suddenly she does say
Mogadishu and
they shot friends in my street
and spoil my country

and my father
he's a teacher
too.

We Please Everyone

This is a shop.
We sell. You buy.
We please everyone, the survivors
and those who plan to do it
properly.

We earn a great deal of money
though few come through the door.
Our shop is empty and silent.
Looking at us you'd think
this is a bad business.

But there's plenty of work
and plenty of noise we just
keep it quiet.
When we turn up
everyone hides.

Hospitals are favoured
providing a long term income
superior to battlefields.

We have exclusive access to
high value real estate
rendered worthless
by our activities.

Though our work should last
a century we make sure
that when you visit
your relative has vanished

and some stranger's dumped on top.
This saves you cash and time
on future visits.

We don't mind if these green acres
littered with rotting stones
are sold off
we work more quickly
with a furnace.

Himmler learnt all he knew
from us.
We run a requested
holocaust for everyone,
we keep the secret

we promise not to tell
what happens and
that it will happen.
There's only one thing
we don't know.

Il Gattopardo

Sometimes I find myself thinking about
how my funeral should be performed
as if it might be a ceremony
I could participate in.

I have described the rituals
to several potential executors.
Their response has been surprise
and questions such as

must it take so long?
Is it legal to burn a corpse in the open?
How do we carry it several miles uphill
where there are no roads?

So I expect my remains will vanish
in the local industrial-scale unit
where the throughput is constant
and the parking terrible.

Only my ashes will make the journey
to Whitemore Down.
In a few days it will have become
another memory for those who came,

as when you leave the cinema
talking intensely about what you have seen,
Claudia's sudden beauty
the blank Sicilian heat

and the Prince's recognition
of what his exhaustion is at the end.
Next day with friends you say,
I saw that film 'Il Gattopardo' last night

and that's it except months later
you see a thin volume in a bookshop
and buy it, a gesture of respect
for all that we forget.

An Albanian

This small boy
standing before me
selling roses
knows no Greek
or English,

holds up
one finger which means
one hundred or one thousand
though he seems indifferent
as to which.

He lives in a van
on the harbour
I saw him through the windscreen
his father's head
in Fagin shadow-play.

I give one thousand
because
he is not only
himself
but also

himself in twenty years
when he will be
hard, bitter, strong
and wish
to kill me.

The Wind And Rain

Another dark morning, all colours in the house
sunk back into the walls, no light
to make them flower.
Rain rustles gently behind the curtains which
when drawn frame the water clustering
and running down the panes against a grey sky
which has come in close.

My back is hurting, what the hell is to be done
about it and about this precious
waking time that is shooting down a drain
into the river into the sea?
Immediately I think of Emily Bronte,
up at seven as always, combing her hair
by the fire, which has flared up
from the embers left overnight.
A December dawn with gales
coming in off the moor.
She's fed Keeper who thinks that next
they should go out over the fields.
But Emily delays doing anything,
her comb's dropped and burnt away.

She doesn't want to go upstairs
and lie down on her bed where she knows
she will have to face once more
that which means to
turn her eyes from the window
against which the wind and the rain tap
and beckon.

Night Rain

Rain is falling on the house
the calm sound
that gives life
the gentle sound
which brings sleep
like a steady rocking
or singing.
That's how it must work.

A Good Place For Next Spring

You don't know me.
I am Philopappos.
Your book says I was born in Syria
and held high offices of state here
in Athens.
When I died my family built this tomb
tall as five men
decorated with scenes from my life.
What I have to say is:
this monument still stands.
Socrates, Plato and all those others
whose lives and works
are better known than mine
are only on the page
but I am on the ground.

I am too old to attract attention,
my lonely pillar on the hill
has become a natural outcrop
chipped, smashed and smoothed
too damaged to provoke more envy.
Only the wind and rain still bother
to try and wear me out.
I will last another thousand years
outlive perhaps all books and memory
and everyone, everywhere.
The lizards will know me
with their feet
and the Autumn swallow will record
a good place
for next Spring.

[The tomb of Philopappus is on the Hill of the Muses, opposite the Parthenon.]

Time Strength Cash Patience

White sky over a field of grass,
cold wind from the hill,
you can see through the hedge
to the horizon.

A lorry drops the load
in the yard,
smooth skin poles
stained green,
deadweight rolls
of wire,
hard thorny bags
of staples.
Then what's needed are
time strength cash patience,
a spade a sledge pickaxe clawhammer
spikes and rods, an auger
and advice.

The hanging stile has a head
a foot or more across.
Pace out half its length
strip back two spade widths
go down a blade deep
stand in the hole
dig out another blade
do it all again
step into the earth
butt the post
against the pit's edge
facing the way
your fence will pull.

Ram soil and rocks
into the hole,
it must tamp down solid
from top to bottom,
so when you raise
the wire across the field
and lever tight
nothing moves
except the fence,
coming up into the wind
like a sail.

It should hold a note
and be as cold and taut
as an iron rail
on a ship.
Rest the gate on bricks between the stiles,
mark off where the iron work
is to go, the spring catch and the hooks,
drill holes then bolt and hammer home.
All who visit now are passengers,
you are on board at the head of the gangway,
even the weather above is yours.

Mrs. Panayiotou's Place

My hotel is on the road by the castle.
The fortress walls surround
large deserted yards
where Franks, Venetians and then
the Turks once killed each other.
We have a tropical garden
in which breakfast is served.
Remember to talk softly
and do not wake the guests
who are sleeping all around you.

One side of the town is the harbour.
You can bathe there, only yachts
drop anchor in the shallows now,
below the ramparts that
stretch away above the sea.
If you take the other turn,
up the hill then right,
there is a bar, a good place
for a drink at sunset as
it faces west, towards Italy.

From its windows you will see
an island called Sapienza
perched over a great pit
beneath the ocean in which
they search all day and night
for whatever time is made of,
using a tower of silver spheres
and stars hidden where the water
is so thick, deep and dark
it is like being buried under a mountain.

I have always lived here,
I take coffee on my verandah
and offer you a cup.
Next year I recommend
a room on the top floor,
as peaceful as the silent
empty castle across the road,
like an ear coiling from the shore
that hears the moon and sky
whisper together along the battlements.

The Songs Of Spring

The dustmen used to sweep the street
after emptying the bins
now the wind does it.

A blackbird perched on a rooftop
sings her song of fear and warning
as my cat waits, indifferent, below

in the middle of the garden
licking his paws
and cleaning his head.

Sitting in the front room I hear
a rising, chattering, shrieking
and in the corridor find the cat

with a fledgling blackbird
in his mouth
which he drops and knocks about

as it scrabbles from wall to wall
across the floor
trying to escape from me.

They never accept rescue.
It lies, eyes clenched, in my hands
heart whirring like a phone

sending a silent urgent message.
I take it out the front
and hide it under a low shrub

hoping its mother will find
and resurrect it, knowing
it will lie there

quivering as if dreaming
and hear the cars,
the crash of the dustmens' truck,

the songs of Spring.

Stepaside

The heartsease is a flower
of the Viola family.
It has purple petals
marked with yellow streaks
like cat's whiskers painted
on a child's face.

It appears in flowerbeds
under hedges
and along the banks of streams
in Spring, but keeps flowering
sometimes into Autumn.

It is wild, self-seeding
and like the violet or primrose
can be cultivated.
Its nodding head blinks in the sun,
early bees which find it
hover, waking up.

In a corner of a valley
there is a place called Heartsease
a few houses and barns
where lanes cross
and hedgerows run away uphill.

The sun flows down and coils
round red brick walls and garden sheds
and forces open upstairs windows.
Heartsease grows everywhere here
where 'Stepaside' is the first house
on the right.

The Inlet

The inlet from above
is shaped like an axe-head
cutting into the splintered
silver rocks along the coast.
Except for us
There is no one here today.

The falcons drive a plover
down into the cove.
They cannot get it easily
because it circles low
over the water.
Then it lands near where we lie
now they have a chance
but do not trust us
to let them take it.

They whip off over the hill
chanting like knives,
*forget it
we can live on air.*

The River Acheron

The river runs clear and green over white rock.
In places it settles in deep pools
or squeezes through tight gaps.
Then you must walk on a path high above the stream
where you can only hear the leap and speed of the water.

Further on it fills a narrow ravine,
cliffs lean over and forest trees cluster
along the water's edge.
You wade against a cold pushing weight
to get on further into the mountains.

The cascade twists and turns like a dropped rope.
We walk for a long time to travel a short way
and check the time to get back safely before dark.
We do not try to reach the spring
high above where the peaks are grey and burnt,
where no one has ever lived
except to hide from their enemies.

The years go by unaccountably fast.
How can it be that this year is almost over?
Since the journey we took last Spring
we have worked and wandered miles
most of it unnoticed even when it was happening.

The Acheron grips your feet
with tireless gleaming hands
and delicate branches drop
a net of light and shadow across your back
which unravels on the river's simmering surface.

The Burning Lake

I'm sorry I could not make out clearly
what you said

when you turned towards me
and looked up

it's just that
I was asleep
and you are dead.

Haunting me wordless
I still see your face

but I know my mind's relentless washing
will make you mortal
twice.

'The Burning Lake':
   Revelations 20: 13-15.

That Man Of Air

A star looks through a bush.
Shade your eyes and more appear
they are still there
you have to kill our light to see them.
I'm told they can be seen
from beneath the sea.
They don't care if we arrange things
so that they can
or cannot be seen
and we don't care either as we
fill sacks with water.

John Keats on his way to Rome
in a small ship with a companion.
Stuck in a cabin, rough weather
all the way just time to write
'Bright Star' then illness
and knowing his brother's fate
is to be his own.

The Spanish Steps are littered
with junkies, lovers and trash.
It was quieter then
and dark enough at night
to see stars in the heart
of the city.
There is no God
but perhaps there is
and he doesn't care
in which case we must hate
that man of air.

Is Light

If we can talk about the cat
or a recent celebration
it means that
what is going to happen
has once more
been deferred.

Midday in winter
the traffic nose to tail
blowing out a mist
which makes the sky white
you can look
straight at the Sun
doused and helpless

like the Moon.
Frank singing
Let's face the music
is full of fight
but getting faint
turn up the volume.

The phone lines are heavy
silted with unsaid
understanding that's why
they hang in loops
above the street
though what we say
is light.

Snakehips

Funerals are cheaper than weddings,
both cost less than a christening.
Snakehips went down like the Wurlitzer
in the ballroom beneath Blackpool Tower
after speeches featuring jokes
made once by the deceased
in the presence of the speaker.
All involved seemed to agree
there was no point in dredging
the depths of grief for words.

We had a few old hits,
Step It Up And Go,
The Midnight Shift, no encore,
then outside in the carpark
a gathering round a pile of flowers
already litter in the gale,
the rain blurred every name.
Somewhere below Snakehips got burnt,
I hope they packed him
sieved and dry
not like something you'd
heel into the gutter.

No invitations, the word goes round,
a note on the board,
an hour off work,
a jar of dust and
a folded card, inside
a photo of a student looking
glad to be alive.
Black cars scatter over London
like beetles from a hole,
put your foot down and drive.

Snakehips leaves a widow,
she shakes and coughs
she did before
but now she'll do it
on her own.
Her future's narrowed
overnight,
the garden's empty
there's no one in the room
or on the phone, *I've
done the gig
I'm coming home.*

Spring In Peckham

The sun beats our jackets off
bare trees look caught out
a pail of daffodils by the door
and the bridal wreath's in flower.

Babies cry, expectant mothers sip
the one drink they're allowed
standing in the garden
you couldn't work last year.

But there are many more to come
your brave widow's
floored and tiled the house
with your lump sum.

Double

When hanging a mirror
it will not allow you
to forget
that someone
is trying to get the levels right.

You pass a door and
glancing in
see yourself
but do not know
who's there

the mirror says
you are not your face
anymore.
That was not always so
at some point

your body
left you behind,
once you knew your twin
now you refuse
your echo,

you are invisible.
In the lobby of the Cumberland Hotel
hookers wait.
The stairs are lined with
sudden frank mirrors.

Shut Down

Move that chair to another room,
throw out the old sofa
stained ten years ago, some
late night incident and
morning row.
We could look for something else
to fill the gap or leave it, get used
to emptiness.

Lights are going out
all over my father' world.
A friend dies in Asia
the continent goes dark,
already Africa has withdrawn
behind the veil
where it shone
when he was young
and closer and closer comes

complete shut down.
Lamps flick off in Kirkby,
London, Hove,
his address book sheds
an inky dust
as words which answered back
in colour once, a daily face,
a Friday night, fear
endured together

go mute
and dry out on the page.
Another walk down
sunken lanes
that remind him of
the Caen bocage.
The sky is clear
and evening comes
like a big room overhead

once full of people singing
but emptying now.
The sun goes down
night falls
a door closing and
as it does a hand
reaches back
and switches off
the light.

My Mother And Her Lover

In Milford Haven
where the subs slide in
my mother tends
the smooth torpedo
and declares it safe.

I was born after
thirty years of war
more wars to come
in a blizzard so white
and thick the ambulance
became invisibly stuck,
the country all out of coals
trying to get up and
clear its head
after deathly blows.

My mother and her lover
with his dripping hands
go on through shining tunnels
towards the blazing hospital
of my life.

Some Time

The clocks have gone back one hour.
This is to rescue dawn from night.
But dawn and dusk
shrink towards each other
just the same.

I sleep with the blinds up
so my room will catch the light
as soon as it comes creeping along the rooftops
like the tide coming in
across a wide dark beach.

The tide rustles like a million skirts.
Dawn is silent
though the pipes tick and knock
and next-door's dog
clears its throat.

The light crowds into the room
insistently, like my father
gently rocking my shoulder
when I was a boy
sleeping on but sure I'd wake

some time.

A Perfect Waste Of Time

Mr. Montano's leisurely brown skin
long fingers indicate
positions on the violin
a rest for tea after half-an-hour
then carefully by spreading
and flicking out the hairs he shows
how to set the tension in the bow.
He took me through the dots
in his high room beside
a smoking road.
If I had listened and also
stuck with him I could now attempt
the Sinfonia Concertante
and feel it in my collar bone.
That would be worth its
price in years
like playing full-back
for a living and
keeping to my coach's line
not giving into fear
of derision, poverty
or decline be
a perfect
waste of time.

London School

A big canvas on every wall of sufficient size.
Grey buildings, brown trees without leaves
soaking parks, black paths
the sky a white backdrop to wet
mid-morning streets and empty afternoon roads
lined with shut villas.
We viewed these respectfully and said
nothing, it was all there
and outside the window too.
But when he retired they sold up
straight away and
after levering the concrete
out of the garden of their new place
he planted vegetables and vines
and drew them
his line growing across the page
like tendrils
and also painted
imagined ceramics, small
jewelled bowls of crimson
blue and emerald and
he found an agent
who sold dozens
in Mexico.

Dripping Eaves

I don't know now why we kept going back
it could have been several things

the long ruined walls like the sides
of a buried ship

black hills of forest climbing up
the earth bare dark and dry beneath,

a fish pond made by monks
the river still dammed and fettered

and a king's grave with flowers
from followers guessing he was there.

Most likely we went for the inn,
not welcoming

after a long cold walk above the valley
but always open

and with few occupants other than
its unsteady owner

reeling white and thin
behind the bar serving

many drinks to himself and you
if you asked, no food

other than eggs out of a giant
bottle of vinegar.

To eat or drink you stood
or sat outside amongst the empties,

broken cars, rubbish and
the old suitcases he'd thrown out

sure they were no use to him
though he stopped the binmen taking them

so they waited there like closed books
beneath the dripping eaves.

The Destruction Of Constantinople

We halt on the ascent
Patmos on the horizon
a cruise liner arcing in
towards Skala.
The sun at ten has
flattened out the sea.
After a pause beneath some stones
we walk down to the cove.

Last year after we'd
given him a melon
Philip sat with us
for a photograph
smiling in his old monk's apron
a plate of blackened figs
crawling with hornets
by his hand.

Each winter
as the storms began
he climbed the mountain
to a chapel
with a well outside
and stayed there
looking west across the Aegean
towards Mystra and Rome.

There are two people here
with a story
about a dying hermit
his chicken sheds empty
and garden dry.
His beard is white
and bigger than the pillow
that his head lies on.

A Vanaprastha In Tufnell Park

He said he'd broken
the habit of a lifetime
and stopped buying
suits and ties.

Cutting back
drawing in
a Vanaprastha
in Tufnell Park.

It's like the end of a holiday.
Use up the lotion shoot off the film
none of it's any use
back home.

[Vanaprastha means 'Forest Dweller', the penultimate stage of life in Hinduism.]

If The Shoaling Sound You Hear

If the shoaling sound you hear
holding a shell to your ear
is not only your own soul's
blood your own soul's tide

but is also the sound of all
the souls who have been betrayed
by a body and have found instead
a home in the sea

deep space on earth that suits
their watery intangibility
if it is their whispering
and sighing too as well as

your own valves' soft tick
the souls of boys who died
running foals on the steppe
girls who sewed for Donatello

an old man ready in this bed
before da Gama came
all hunters fallen in crevasses
the man killed for an insult

down Railton road last week
all of them and the rest
an oceanic that is a vast
but not infinite choir

and like the ocean and
all choirs singing one song
together the first question
must be what are they singing

next is there a conductor
then are they following a score
as whales do or improvising
as humans do like a 50's

quintet steering down
the rapids and cascades
of music that they make
on their way to the delta

where the music stops?

On The Beach

Why is the sea cool
at the surface
warm below
as if it's
upside down?

A stream
comes from the mountain,
crosses fields
where farmers
look after it,
is allowed
beneath the road,
hurries though groves
of oak and juniper
in which chameleons
hesitate,
spills between shadows
onto the bay's
dazzling gold
blue mask
and floats.

This trickle
chills your skin,
come out,
sit by the stump,
see girls parade
along the beach
from the campsite
to the town
while waiting
for night,
their backs will bend
like they've got no bone.

We'll lie here,
the sun has warmed
our patch,
sand cushions your hips,
let your book's spine break.

The Way Home

We bought a place in a country where
farmers would sometimes go into their barns
and hidden in the bales shoot themselves.
The hedges left so long unlaid
big oaks stood up in lines.

Tommy told us not to let the *didicoi*
get close enough to lean on the gate.
When I paid for the ground in cash
gave back some notes, *luck money*
he said, *you'll need that here*.

Fields and woods along steep hillsides,
farms divided from each other by lanes
rising to a house, the sky over all
holding down the hill day after day
the same silent horizon.

Working the sheds and pastures,
across the moorland with a dog,
their calls and the lapwing's echo
solitary, clear and certain.
We sat in a window to hear them
finding the way back home.

The Open Door Into The Garden

A hot day, London like Rome,
tables out, coffee and exhaust.
It used to rain and we ate at home
with the door shut
never in the street.
Now doors and windows are
unlocked until late
and my mother's here
who lived in London once
when it was not Rome.

At first she refused the little frame
but now his head is firm
upon his shoulders
she takes him, his soft limbs
filling out for the long run to come.
Her thin fingers hold him
in a net, the flesh that smoothed
her silhouette consumed
getting along this final stretch.
They are together in the kitchen,
she holds him on her lap
as he stares out into the room then
lifts his head to wonder at her
old grey brow bowed over,

and as we watch this
sacred implacable truth
the door into the garden is open
so the breeze will carry
warm air from the stove
away upstairs and out of
windows high up in the roof
where it vanishes with everything
that's said or heard
or touched or seen.

Words Of Fire

A bolt of lightning entered
the house via
a seagull
all the sockets blew
out of the walls an
incandescent orb
hovered at
knee height
in the kitchen
she fled through
the back door
fell over the
corpse unplucked like
a bundled
feather boa
and waited
for the windows to shed
tears of fire
the slates to flash
red and silver tablets but
the place sat still a
little smoke
crept by her toes
as she
looked in
where did it go?

nothing becomes nothing
perhaps the massive
rocks below
trapped it
or the bed frame holds
a hot surprise or
if you open this book
one day instead of words
better the sun
in miniature will float
above the page as
the print glittering
flies back
through the roof.

Somewhere To Go

All harbours are beautiful
full of iron and space

their own horizon
and a dome of light.

At Mandraki beneath the windmills
we sat above the oily blue

with its slight fine air
of salted sewage

looking at the great walls
before the city

the liners and tankers
yachts from Hamilton

gin palaces from Ostia
fishing boats poking about

for a place
the arriving, leaving

and waiting.
Then, walking up the lane

behind the kiosks and go-downs
we found a shop just shutting

and bought green olives
a lump of bread some apricots.

Back on deck waiting
you were tired and bored

Is this what you've been
going on about?

But the sea is calm
around our white bow

the luggage stacked
our captain idles.

Beyond the point
the north wind

which blows all summer
is making the hydrofoils

bellyflop and crawl
this is the best place to be

always, bags packed and
somewhere to go.